In Memory of the Fast Break

In Memory of the Fast Break

Michael Sweeney

Plain View Press
P. O. 42255
Austin, TX 78704

plainviewpress.net
sb@plainviewpress.net
1-512-441-2452

Cover art: Deborah Dutko

for Patricia

Thanks to Beverly Boehmke, Mike Bozzone, Marian Calabrese, Yolanda Cartusciello, Ralph and Judy Corrigan, David Curtis, Deborah Dutko, Bill Evans, Sid Gottlieb, Karen, Joe, and Michael Grasso, Mary Ellen and Gene Kendall, Janet Krauss, Linda O'Brien, Robin McAllister, Nick and Jackie Rinaldi, Tony Sanders, Joanna Sit, Michele Madigan Somerville, Susan Fromberg Schaeffer, Robert, Michelle, and Erin Sweeney, Therese Sweeney, Patricia Sweeney, Annette Sczcesiul, the late Allen Ginsberg, and especially my parents, the late James and Mary Sweeney, and my brothers, the late James Neville Sweeney Junior and the late William Patrick Sweeney.

Acknowledgments

The following poems first appeared in the publications listed below:

"When Giants Walked the Earth," "Homage to the Dave Clark Five," *Gulf Stream Magazine* (No. 2, 1990); "Last Poem for Robert," *Chase Park* (Volume I, Number 2, 2001); "Wreckreational," *Phantasmagoria* (Volume I, Number 2, 2002); "How Benjy Saw Rodney King," *Red Brick Review* (1995); "Hank Gathers Threw it Down," *The Oval Magazine* (Spring 1996); "Quarrys Don't Quit," *Half Tones to Jubilee* (Fall 1996); "Shoeless Joe Died for Our Sins," *Sport Literate* (Spring 1997); "Why I Write About Sports," *Blue Mesa* (Fall 1997); "Duet: Too Late to Stop Now," *Southern Poetry Review* (Spring 1998); "Cold Pastoral," *TMP Irregular* (Spring 1999); "Allen Ginsberg's Sneakers," *Thin Air* (Volume III, Number 2, 1998); "Cry of its Occasion," *The Southern Anthology* (Summer 1998); "Further," *Eclipse* (Fall 2001); "Big Pink's For Sale," *ProCreation* (Volume 3, Number 1, 1999); "In Memory of the Fast Break," *Prairie Star* (Winter, 1999); "Black Bears in White Hills," *The Larcom Review* (Fall/Winter, 2000); "Robert, You Write About Things," *Wavelength* (Number 2, Spring, 2001); "Waving Goodbye With Your Fist," *Natural Bridge* (Number 11, Spring 2004); "Belly of the Beast," *The Ledge* (Number 28, Spring-Summer 2005); "Chorus: Out of this Place, *The Lucid Stone* (Spring 1995); "Monster Lament," *The Ledge* (Number 30, Fall/Winter 2007); "The Last Cracker," *Margie* (Volume Six, Fall 2007); "Desperate Schemes of Offensive Linemen," *Four Corners* (Number 4, Fall 2006).

Contents

Part One

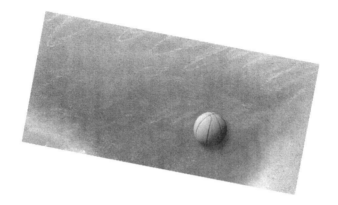

It is very happily and kindly provided, that in every life there are certain pauses and interruptions, which force consideration upon the careless, and seriousness upon the light; points of time where one course of action ends and another begins; and by vicissitude of fortune, or alteration of employment, by change of place, or loss of friendship, we are forced to say of some thing, "this is the last."

Samuel Johnson, *The Idler* (5 April 1760)

First Time Over the Rim

That instant my calves twitched
as I came off that baseline pick –
just a stab of daylight
to the lane before me – I felt
in the air before my cut,
my left foot splashing the half-
frozen puddle but the right one
coming down hard on dry asphalt
& pushing off, up through
March sunlight splintered against
the chainlink fence, above the whir
of elbows & hips like I'd
never quite be again I caught
the lob gratefully with my
two small hands

When Giants Walked the Earth

They stood out even through the static, rabbit ears bent
on the old Zenith, plastic whipped from the window panes

staple by staple: arthritic Russell barely twitching his beard
toward the inbounds pass, Reggie Harding leaning with him

just as Russell soars the other way, catching the lob
two feet above the rim & jamming it – the old dummy play! –

poor Harding all the while standing there scratching his head
like he must have ten years later, strung out on a neighborhood stoop,

right before some like joker blew off his scalp with a .38:
Russell never letting up – young bloods he'd locked hips with

in the pivot worn down each March, gasping for second wind
from Syracuse to Fort Wayne: names buried deeper than old gyms

under the wrecking ball, their Converse prints alongside Big Bill's –
making himself sprint back on defense as the crowd roared so hard

they shook pigeons from Cobo Hall's rafters, we felt it
in Boston on our blinking screen: a wind gust rumbling east

through the Rust Belt that kicked on our furnace all by itself.
Dad shivered "Jesus, look at them go! But what else can they do?"

Shoeless Joe Died for Our Sins

I loathe *Field of Dreams* even more than *The Big Chill* –
loathsome dupes, playing for tears, singing "Joy to the World"
to their kids, wash away their sorrow till they almost drown
in soapy bubbles, oldies radio world without end. Loath-
some agenda you can't escape, Dutch Reagan broadcasting
how it was from Ann Arbor to Dubuque barely above
a croak – *all the world's a film, you're captured forever*
as you never were, each grainy frame in your brain
airbrushed clean. Let Joe Jackson play in your yard,
ornery & spry as when young Dick Daley sneaked
through the turnstiles into another world, let him say
what you want to hear – *old man Comiskey done me wrong*
but that don't mean I hadda lay down. Man put his mark
on the dotted line gotta play like an eight year old
proud as Hell of his first callus, hopin' the sun don't
ever go down. Lord I swear I'd shag flies for nothin'
if that kid believe it ain't so. Hear that Southside kids
& even you can play – shed no tears that Comiskey Park's
dead as your neighborhood, it will rise again!, soon as
fathers you never had get up whole from the street,
dust off chalk marks cops drew around them & show
how you grip a bat. Anything goes in America,
greatest country ever was.

Belly of the Beast

Nothing from scrimmage no brokenfield runs on sod trodden into dirt,
can't get traction anywhere but swivel those creaky hips, still gotta feed
the beast, Earl Campbell nowadays barely climbs into his truck but brother
you're not there yet, pump those arthritic knees, somebody's always after
you to fuck up & blame yourself. Rod Shoate haunts the Combat Zone
under the Hunter's Moon after Longhorns & Buffalo Bills, one more blind-
side hit, all Mike Webster recollects out in the rain & snow after thousands
of perfect snaps, tackles that realign your bones, the gray matter coiled in
your skull, after Three Rivers & Schaeffer implode you still gotta feed
the beast. *No memory of having starred atones for later disregard or keeps
the end from being hard:* John Unitas just last month couldn't bend over
a putt but you can still *Go to work. Crush people. Get paid. You gotta
love this job.* Even the semipro New England Stars need fodder for special
teams, Korey Stringer fell against that white Minnesota heat but you
gotta push downfield, nary a backwards glance– there's thundering cleats
on the killing floor, lowing & frozen stream, they'll pelt you with ice-
balls & half-empty Coors from East Boston concrete stands but don't
bet against the spread, it's always 4th & ten, way down the foodchain
& long in the tooth you hustle to feed the beast

for my brother Robert,
semi-pro football, age 43

Hank Gathers Threw It Down

Bo Kimble also ran in Knickerbockerland,
  no more life of Riley, no commemorative
lefty freethrows garbagetime or not, no more
  Westhead Shakespeare soundbites tomorrow
or tomorrow or tomorrow; L Train also ground
  it out March asbestos nights back through
icejams, tremors, mud, roads collapsing
  underfoot like warped Palestra rims bent
in another life, another Reggie's embryonic
  praying mantis jay aborted near Dunbar
sure as the sun ariseth through asphalt haze
  sans adjectives, *sans* adrenaline, *sans*
even escape velocity, the very idea
  you burn out but not yet

In Memory of the Fast Break

Nothing astounding under the sun after you'd been knocked down
& elbowed your way back under the rim after the ball came off. If you
were taller or wanted it more you'd grab it with both of your hands,
& wasn't that little Pete Ragucci already taking off one step ahead of
his wife

Unseld barely left his feet but even Gus Johnson said if there's a rebound
we just have to grab, we know in our hearts that Wesley will get it, Unseld
wider than Boerwinkle now, that cannonball outlet pass

Don't turn your back on Beaver Smith, who'd whip the ball off your head
fast as he later hijacked cars & left those souls maimed in his wake, nothing
but asphalt & exhaust, don't let your teammates down

None of 'em had a chance, Earl the Pearl Monroe stripped like a mark
by Sam Jones, halfcourt, midswivel, Sam laughing all the way back

"I would have all young people taught to respect themselves, the rights
of others, and all sacred things…": Albert Parlin's "Character" chiseled
in bonewhite cement wide as a movie screen in front of his junior high.
Who hadn't copied the whole damn speech in discipline after school,
ream after ream of platitudes while everyone else was in gym, "Character"
egged each Halloween, Krylon aerosol paint, quick now, here now,
footfalls down Everett streets

None of 'em had a chance, Big E hitting that turnaround jay, token
pressure from Russ, but next time Big Bill got in his shirt, tipping
the ball to himself as the other Celts broke downcourt. Every touch
afterward E would just heave it so hard he nearly broke glass, Russell
cackling from the bench, jai alai garbagetime

Twenty years later & decades ago Ginsberg pissed at you yet again asked
if a billion odd Chinese knew who Bill Russell was. They do now & too
bad for them: legions of scrawny boys & girls running in layup drills
or stitching Nike-wear faster than they can afford, either a coach or an
overseer, just do it no matter what

Thought you'd outrun anything inside Edith Street Park's WPA stone
walls, chase each other baseline & back then drink till your bellies sagged,
tongues like winded hounds, water dribbling funky as sweat from the
wrought iron fountain spout even as shades of the prison close upon
fastbreaking growing boys. Manslaughter, murder, molestation: panting
pubescent kids ground into tabloid fare for crimes beyond your grasp,
with a gun butt, with a shovel, behind classroom doors: Barry walks
deadpan, shackled & cuffed on "America's Most Wanted" like he
knows his way back to Walpole, like Thoreau almost coughed up blood
when he wrote in an unjust state the only place for a just man is prison.
Moriarty, Macauda, Puopolo: none of 'em had a chance

Who can you trust to do the right thing out in the open court when
Hardaways like Penny & Tim walk the ball up like mules

Dreamt John Havlicek died last night while Riley got born again,
sworn to dish out everything he took from Adolph Rupp, proud he
once ate Hondo's dust, so hopeless he nearly puked, but that was
thirty years ago & look at the Garden now: three quarters rubble
with innards exposed & gaping like primeval worms in North
Station's grimy light. "Red always said if you have to pass
the ball around four or five times it was a bad play to begin
with," but now the old Garden's gone except for the parquet
floor

Bill Russell's Shadow

The Garden yawned as Marques Haynes
dribbled through the New Jersey Rens
over dead spots in the parquet floor,
the Garden half-filled, holding in
winters of smoke & sweat as ushers
blocked aisles to the half court seats
& gangly kids growing out of crew cuts
inhaled bad popcorn in the tunnels,
kids like me killing time before
the real game when that cackle
ricocheting down the hallway turned
our heads toward the shadows coming
at us, we held our breaths as the two
of them emerged, a woman whose
blue eyes pierced the darkness, quick
little steps, Russell himself no wider
than his shadow as he breezed by
still laughing, ebony cane with
his black cape trailing behind,
adjusting his stride to hers so easy
we felt it down to our sneakers,
me the tallest up to his shoulder
blades thanking God for the sense
to look away

Monster Lament

    Once they could hit you we drove you off like some kind
of human being, nobody's hands were clean, something awful
early on soured our afternoons worse than all the bitter milk
we sucked from our mothers' teats. The bullpen cart would lurch
so bad we had to align the wheels after each bleak homestand,
rain slanting north-northeast, Aprils when Fenway was one-
quarter full & Converse ran graveyard shifts. What dumb creature
comes back for more hounded by every slight Sal Maglie left
unavenged when he headhunted on his own, baleful stiff-legged
strides off the mound baring those yellow teeth, arms raised
higher than either Klitschko after you'd punch 'em out. Some-
thing monstrous in us all blamed you for breaking down when
that was your destiny since Callison took you deep way back
at windy Shea, doomed to expire near four hundred pounds,
limbs swollen purple & black, you that dragged Mantle under
.300 all by your nasty self. You were born to pulverize what-
ever we'd deign to hate & those were relentless days whenever
you got the ball – always that barking after you, pitchforks &
splintered bats since Albert DeSalvo was loose not half a mile
from our door, since the Remains played *Diddy Wah Diddy*
& Landsmark was on the ground prone & impaled with a flag,
since we roared *Tessie* with torches aloft before there was
Yawkey Way, roaming down avenues never condemned,
paved over & gentrified. You can get petrified looking back,
nothing's more damn grotesque, but I recall an 0-2 changeup
froze a young Boog Powell
Dick Radatz (1937-2005)

Wreckreational

"shooting perfect jumpers by ourselves at the only backboard with no rim"

Just as well there isn't a rim, you're lucky enough to hit glass
wind at your creaky back, & don't even dream about throwing
it down, you're liable to fall as hard as a stumblebum so out-
classed he's dropped by some phantom jab that can't crack
a hardboiled egg, you don't have a puncher's chance, stuck
inside this chainlink fence with your George Mikan ABA ball
punctured for thirty years, you can't miss without a rim but
make sure to keep your head up as you uncoil a finger-roll
off your wrong foot after how many highlight reels of Iceman
& Dr.J. (*damn!*): when nobody's game outlandish enough
to measure up in the end just post up your younger self with
any lame moves you've got left, fallaway jumpers & wind-
mill hooks that Russell made obsolete but this isn't fantasy
camp – that fresh kid's just cut off the baseline & taken your
dropstep away, he'll swat the ball right back in your teeth
& cradle the ricochet like it was always his, faster than any-
thing you can recall he's cutting down nylon nets like he'll
never wind up in your shoes, inside this chainlink fence,
wind at his creaky back. Like he's not in your face again
dribbling it all away

for Tony Sanders

Celtics' Last Stand

All the rims are thirty feet high & baselines are half a mile wide,
while yet another heavy-legged point guard walks the ball upcourt.
What can dyspeptic Celtics do but fume & regurgitate? Earl Strom
bit the dust in 1994, malignancy in the brain, how many drunken
anathemas to conjure Tim Donaghy? Cousy sold his memorabilia
to help his daughters out. You can get Russell's autograph for less
than Shaquille O'Neal's simply by clicking a mouse. Walter Brown,
my miserable brethren, ain't walking through that door. Danny's
finally mortgaged the future, so listen to Johnny Most dogwhistle
from beyond on the Shuttlesworth-KG years. Bones McKinney
never reached the rafters in his dreams. Red grew more apocryphal,
cantankerous & uncouth, hobbling to his seat past the millennium;
now mere pigeons disrespect the statue at Faneuil Hall. Dennis
Johnson just collapsed outside the Austin gym he found himself
exiled to. Every rim's collapsible but you can still shatter glass.
Marvin Barnes got busted again & nobody's seen King Rat
up in the new mezzanine. Reggie Lewis last I heard
rests in an unmarked grave

Desperate Schemes of Offensive Linemen

What kind of terror makes you flinch when you're three hundred pounds

What encroachment what bold stunts what Foxboro safety blitz drawn up
    inside a cave somewhere near Kandahar

What great plumage spooks your kid after your helmet's on & your
    facemask's so byzantine he can't see your hazel eyes

What outlandish old fatigues strung out in the wind bring a lump
    to your throat

Whither the fabled power sweep bituminous afternoons over hardscrabble
    provinces stampeded into dust since Carlisle took Syracuse

What the fuck does chronic traumatic encephalopathy say

What grim anonymity back in the phalanx again when nobody's broken
    ranks & your quarterback's still not sacked

What indigenous buffalo couldn't be any more gone

What known leg-whip or crack-back block saves you a dressing-down
    worse than a flogging at Riyadh or a stoning outside Cheyenne

What kind of hunger drove you back to shuffle & sniff around here

What acute contingency when there's no weight-bearing bone or tendon
    or reattached ligament martyrs can't rupture or snap

What fanatical leverage keeps the chains moving north

What poor camaraderie down in a naked scrum once you hear
    unmuzzled dogs & your sphincter can't hold its load

What kind of pussy training camp when no one drops dead in the heat

What made you hit the blocking sled falling apart in your yard after your
    veteran ass got waived & the bank took your restaurant

What growth hormones shrank your balls smaller than sun-dried grapes

What dementia drove you to torch that chicken processing plant

What made you smuggle your weight in dope back across Interstate 10

What grotesque extremities left you to stagger & claw down at
    Guantanamo

What unholy menstrual blood smeared on your week-old beard

What made you pump the Taser then into your wasted thigh as sirens bore
    into your skull & all you can see are trees

What made you guzzle antifreeze where the three rivers converge

What kind of creature will rise up & crawl from carpet-bombed monoliths
    imploded stadiums onion-domed arsenals

What residual friendly fire lodged in Pat Tillman's corpse

What strange cadence what new count what audibles barked in Greek
    after the last headslap

We must evolve as human beings out of a three-point stance

Kung Fu Redux

Even wisest man grows tense
With some sort of violence
           Yeats

Rip Van Carradine goes through the motions
   humble as the dust, off the freeway
still on his feet twenty years down the road,
   Murdoch's generic urban frontier bad
as it ever gets but grasshopper's spry, his
   blue eyes glitter even while wiseass
knucklehead scumbags crumble like half-
   baked bricks, thrustkicks & palmheels
when all else fails & all else always does:
   vengeance begats virulent bastards
week after bloody week worse than a god-
   damn plague, & Caine's seen enough
hysterical women whose sons lay wasted
   & maimed to last the millennium, they
never fucking learn: syndicated hemorrhaging
   can't revive Saint Bruce Lee, never
a gentle man, Brandon stiffens underground
   without a second take to cast a
colder eye on epitaphs worse than his,
   gauntlets Kwai Chang's yet to run
like katas in his sleep stoned out of
   his skull: ridgehand to temple, snap-
kicks murder on the toes, to be continued
   till he wakes or breaks up his lines
in *Kill Bill*, whichever comes first

Long Hard Slog

And then it got downright treacherous, you'd fall in a pangee trap or trip off
a roadside bomb dormant since Mossadegh, back out of all this now, you
weren't there so you don't know from O'Brien or Stephen Crane, fatigue
makes cowards of us all but now you've got orders to march, all of this

now too much, you gotta move that blocking sled maybe another ten yards,
there's ploughboys encrusted with shrapnel & mud that quicken again near
Verdun like creatures from *Ghosts of Mars*, sniffing for mustard gas, hear
the Dead sing *Black-Throated Wind* as they rip off their old fatigues,

whole again beyond confusion into the bloody breech, you weren't there
so shut the fuck up & get your ass back in line, you can eat horseflesh
at Stalingrad hunched till your wet fur froze, you can burn rubber at
Myanmar, they're cooling LeBron James soles on castiron mobile racks,

you can find quarrel in a straw when honour's at the stake, drink & be
whole again, here's to the quagmires & rebel yells, staggering bygone days,
all those Patriots bumping chests sacking stout Jake Delhomme, back when
the blood ran ankle-deep & the sledded Poles were smote over an angry
word,

back when they plowed your fields with salt & dragged your man through
the dust outside of windy Troy, back by the rivers of Babylon when your
gods were surly & young, back when your knuckles scraped the earth
& you couldn't tell left from right

The Wellfleet Whale

Bruce said that kata's like swimming on land
Some mean karaoke & air guitar
You're helpless except for your empty hand

Those fantasy jams with the E Street Band
It's hard to remember just where you are
Bruce said that kata's like swimming on land

What did Blake see in that granule of sand
Seiuchin will get you only so far
Better try reading the palm of your hand

Stagger through sanchin until you can't stand
There's always another badass to spar
It never was easy swimming on land

Deconstruct poems at your sensei's command
That slovenly wilderness in a jar
Nobody falls for that old sleight of land

But Kunitz's Wellfleet Whale's on the strand
What could you witness more sad & bizarre
If you can spend decades swimming on land
Imagine extending your empty hand

Your Worthy Opponent

Got no satin robe, what's staring you down, not even socks –
just black trunks & high tops, eyes deader than Muhammad Ali's

last time Trump led him through the ropes, barked *wave, Champ*:
shuffle! Nineteen inch neck & a pulse so sluggish all things

within twenty feet seem to crawl. Ten ounce gloves like you.
Stare back for Christ sake, get past what smolders behind

those dim pupils, its very own dream of a perfect night –
kidney shots that make you piss blood, legs folding as you're hit

twice more on your way down (roars from all sides
like they're clubbing you themselves, the assholes! Closest

they'll ever get to your street's wobbling down the Boardwalk
puking shrimp cocktail), that thud on the canvas

you won't even feel, irises rolling back of your skull –
what bores down on every naked one of us. Michael

empty your mind – there's no telling, once the bell rings,
just no telling what a young man can do

Quarrys Don't Quit

No matter who you think you are you're beaten in the end, always
what you never see lacerates you worse than any Ali jackhammer jab
knocking in your ears decades after the scar tissue heals & you squint

at your brother Mike, even worse than Smokin' Joe doubling up on
those hooks underneath your ribs & flush on your naked jaw like
you went skidding misaligned, broadsided by a truck, worse

than your father's litany that "Quarrys never quit" drilled so deep
in your skull you stagger backwards like his words still throb
like that bloody nose, the other kid's knobby fist swollen & scraped

as yours – never saw yourself so proud you couldn't lace your shoes
or hum along with your peers in a ring at the convalescent home,
songs that echo so far down you'd rather get the bends, where Queer

Street's just a cul-de-sac & memory's a vice tight as your mother
hugging you now or a Floyd Patterson clinch, who the hell knows which
– what you belted out by heart in your Confirmation robes as a light-

weight ready to fight for Christ & shrug off the bishop's slap like
it was Don King's outstretched hand, grimace & bear it no matter what,
no matter who you ever were they get you in the end

Waving Goodbye with Your Fist

Hang around anyplace long enough they tear it down where you stand,
don't look back or they drag you under, swearing you own 'em *large*,
you worthless ungrateful wretch, let your grievances go, let 'em resound
like so many kiais back in the SHU Box gym just when they shut it down,
nets unstrung from collapsible rims, rims unscrewed from the glass, back-
boards pried from the stanchions themselves & banners a decade unread
gone from their sooty walls like bricked-over windows entombed, nothing's
beyond recall, back when our vagabond Isshinryu dojo watched you do
kusanku for maybe the thousandth time, you know better than me, watched
you bow alone into darkness, searching with empty hands till you strike
out fast with your left, but there's no rush, you slow it down, gripping
the hardwood floor as you parry each phantom attack like you saw 'em
for what they are, Salvadoran deathsquad thugs once & for all dispatched
with a snapkick or elbow strike, sanctimonious venal suits stealing behind
your back get the ball of your callused foot as you wheel around in midair
before they can even flinch, talk about bottom line, it's that simple in
the kata, you can stop time itself with a straightforward vertical punch
right out of taikyoku one, twenty years back when your front two knuckles
broke against grainy air & your kiai woke comatose dogs chained in
their scraggly yards either end of Park Ave., man you were so intense,
but you saw then how they'd fold up the bleachers even before you'd
bow out, open palm over fist, just one soul in his own Okinawa ready
to start sunsu like you were almost there, *that's* the spirit, that
very next crescent step

        for sensei Ralph Corrigan,
        retiring from teaching

Stagmire

Little Carmine Lupertazzi's gotten away with words, Frankie Valli's
his consigliere, his villa's a faux Versails but he's just his father's son,
already dug his grave, locked in a fragmire sotto vox with coldlidded

Johnny Sack. Even wisest man grows tense with some sort of violence,
Yeets hit it right on its head, occupational hazards abound feral in tooth
& claw – doomed Joe Peeps on Cherry Hill Road wild to be wreckage

forever, mangled Stealth bombers like Ottoman steeds bleeding on Raven
Plain, Hummers upended & burning at Storrs, Fallujah & Port-au-Prince,
absolute slagmire there, ridden of meddlesome Creole priests with ordnance

from friends of ours. Carmine could use those gentlemen post hasty if not
before, what's done unto others is done, they've loosed the wolves back into
the wild all over Yellowstone, packs of 'em after dumbfounded elk that

gnaw on the greasy grass, the Esplanade of Science & Trucking's liable
to get hit next & who can you sacrifice, who's gonna lug that goddamn
cross backwards to Abu Ghraib, who knocked Butkus on his ass & dragged

the rest downfield, slaughtered indigenous buffalo couldn't be any more gone,
caught the Swingin' Neckbreakers live back at the Crazy Horse & ducked
under friendly fire, wailing & gnashing abroad, all grotesque forsaken

things naked & trembling again, lammed it up to Gobblers' Notch on
lifted New Hampshire plates, live free or die motherfucker, it's a stagmire
just like he said, it's every man for himself

Last Poem for Robert

Barely a game between us then even
before the wind got louder at Riverview Park,
our last one-on-one, brothers either end of our
forties backing each other down like we still
had a shot, each long rebound blown offcourt
almost over the ledge & into the Housatonic,
brutal chasing 'em down, barely held our pivot
foot whacking at flesh & bone anywhere foul-
line in, our last one-on-one, on your flailing
baseline drive I slapped you upside your head,
no blood no foul, you climbed over my creaky
back bulging disc be damned after the ball came
loose, what did we have to lose?, stranger than
spastic dribbling fools under that toxic sky,
looked like a funnel touching down maybe near
Stevenson Dam but that game was all we had,
after the scraggly leaves kicked up whirling
like Earl Monroe, your repossessed camper
on cinder blocks gone up the Merrimack,
the rock garden you built yourself against
your adrenaline deep in New Hampshire sand,
nothing stood between us then as the rain hit
that asphalt court, awful & awesome at once,
our last one-on-one, taking it to the rim
just above our reach

Cowboy Down

Stumble home. Get angry. Cross the threshold standing up
& thank George W. Bush all your storm windows are down –
sun's already gone before five, furnace kicked on by itself,
you could hit fungos with those tomatoes frozen hard over-
night. How many moons since you ran to the park with your
lefty MacGregor glove unoiled & barely strung, those last few
acres of open space fallow as Wounded Knee, what would
you finally sacrifice to bury that ancient angst? Hunt down
Buckner in Idaho for all that you can't make right this bitter
November dusk, for all those lights going off in the sky far
back as Babylon – what sounds like thunder's just some machine
let loose on someone else, makeshift Hummers & donkey carts
not even smithereens. Vengeance means making the selfrighteous
crawl & you want to grip a bat like you never left fantasy camp,
every cliché is true – Pedro punches Posada out & Pesky guns
Slaughter down, Saddam catches a live grenade lobbed down
his spiderhole but you're flashing back to Detroit, still can't erase
that frame, Aparacio falls down again just as he's rounding third.
There's no one, brother, bad enough to get what they deserve –
we're all of us wasted & maimed. Stop lacerating yourself.
Cross the threshold without a throw & get off
that goddamn horse

November 2003

39

". . . humanely destroyed 10-4-89"

When thoroughbreds dream their blinders drop off, Secretariat
left alone to lie down before noon, nineteen years galloping back

hard as he used to charge himself even lifetimes after Belmont,
still the joker at Claiborne Farm, scaring the Hell out of starstruck slobs

who drop their carrots before he veers off: stud like that had to explode
soon as his paddock door sprung open, every mare they backed him into

never felt muscles so tensed: three hundred foals & not one with his twitch,
that drive to break free & eat up turf till no hooves echo but his:

Lord how we kept up one long roar every inch of the stretch, shits
our own mothers wouldn't trust to cash their Social Security

ripping our tickets for shame – who'd ever think we'd still remember
a dumb animal's stride? He must too, as he kicks in his sleep:

New York in bloom, absolute scum ennobled, even Richard phlebitis Nixon
thinking he'd never get caught! No one's so lame he can't rear back &

feel what he was born to that cold March day, barely dropped from Something-
royal but up & wobbling, his first snortful of dust

Why I Write About Sports

> Time past and time future
> What might have been and what has been
> Point to one end, which is always present
>
> Eliot, "Burnt Norton"

He's back again & breathing hard, lumbering down the lane
something like Antoine Carr on a career night: it's his ball

& he's not looking back unless he's about to fake another
outrageous lookaway pass to Vlade Abdul Jabbar who'd throw

it down without breaking stride but he's not giving it up:
always time to compensate when your game's so old you even

fool yourself, that syncopated chest-high dribble crying out
to get swiped ever since Larry Havlicek ripped off Isiah Greer

but he's no Reggie Maravich blindsided on the fly & nailed to
some parquet floor, at least not yet: Showtime's just

a layup drill nobody figures out till they fall back in line,
Silk Ceballos rides again trailing the break downcourt as

the sun goes down on the Great Western Forum, what else can you do
but finish off from where you start & put back each last shot,

what rolls off the rim again & hangs there like before forever
past their reach, every time they play it back you leave 'em

where they were, all those Warriors eating your dust flatfooted
faceless & bald: ask Joe Smith in fifty years

for Magic Johnson

High Above Courtside

Poetry's when Jungle Jim never once elbowed or tripped hatchetmen
  like Harry the Horse or RoughHouse Rudy La Russo
when Bobby Jones would loosen your teeth faster than Clyde Lovellette
  Big Clyde who hogged it at garbagetime, screw you Siggy too
when Walter Brown remortgaged his house & swallowed hard on faith
  Big Bill bent his arthritic knees & Nellie's prayer came down
when van Breda Kolff stuck with Counts & dammed all those balloons
  Big Red made Kareem suck wind & *hit the fucking post!*
when stout Sid Borgia stuck it to Red who stuck in Willie the Whale
  stuck Vitale with Mc Adoo, stuck by K.C. Jones
when Selvy pulled up baseline & missed & *Havlicek stole the ball!*
  wiped that smirk off Isiah's puss, made McFilthy snarl
when Tree bit Danny & Wilt chased Sam & *Laimbeer tomohawked Chief!*
  whacked poor Larry's coccyx bone, stepped on Kevin's foot!

Running tales for growing boys who never learned to jam crackling
  like third rail static either end of the Orange Line
Dudley brothers & Thompson Square Townies their ears pressed close
  like going down avenues never condemned, paved over
& gentrified, not a goddamn chance, Rapid Robert's dribbling
  like it's nineteen fifty three while northeast winds
still rasp off water to make the Standells gag, so rave on
  like Krapp right down to your last parochial croak
blacker Irish transistor strains than Moses or Sam Malone
  like gargling razor blades forty years till nothing
drowns you out, not even trains rumbling home to North Station
  like Wide Wayne down the lane for one more shot,
one last gob of phlegm, high above courtside, nothing
  like it while it lasts, spat on McNasty's grave

Johnny Most (1923-1993)

Part Two

Hence I became eventually, gradually, unashamed of my mind's incapacity, just
    as I had once written
Poems to be read many times, but what was the use of that? Now I write poems
    to be read once and forgotten,
Or not to be read at all.

Hayden Carruth

Exile, Silence, Cunning

Why not call it cowardice & sentimentality beneath
those sublunar antithetical passive-aggressive masks?
Thus go the bloody gallowglass antlered & heavy-armed
back to the old stone fort, such that don't lightly quit
the fielde, but byde the brunt to the end for some venal
chieftain's sake. Clan of the boar & battle-axe, brothers
to hardnesse & cold, ready to shear off a horseman's leg
& level the scrawny horse with the same ruthless blow –
how many legends spawned like mad through long nights
of soaking rain? Why not call it endurance & stealth
as they waited the norsemen out in hovels unfit for dogs,
mouthing our sad apocrypha through jagged & rotting
teeth? Thus Cuchulain stitching shrouds with dastardly
bird-throated shades after he slaughtered waves knee-
deep off Bailie Strand, swear upon fealty foot!, bright-
headed *ceallach* signifies strife on our maternal side,
Saint Patrick's slavelord awful Naill Mor whose son
kissed the celtic cross, crazy Suibhne gone astray into
the stunted trees absent his shirt of mayle – how many
grand embellishments these squalid millennia? We've
been well-going since Robert the Bruce drove us from
Castle Sween soon after Bannockburn, cast into sagas
of headlong rout & westward diaspora – ape-neck barbers
fallen down drunk & knockabout lumberjacks lost in
Algonquin woods, hawk-nosed provos & sundry pogues
slumming near Winter Hill, squatters & sandhogs &
adjunct hacks anonymous as the sod where all of us
decompose on top of our restless dead soon as we
first draw breath. They're still cracking Saxon skulls
& kicking their fucking brains back in the Irish Sea
if that's what we realize, but we've no axe that's keen
enough to follow men like them. Why not call it artifice
& unbridled lunacy once they grow so passing strange
we strain to pronounce their names?

Bill Nolan's Antique Blues

Whole decades gone wrong, all sorts of nice kids chasin'
that Liverpool saltwater taffy with Motown near beer –
no wonder their bellies ache! Crackheads howlin' down

Seaside Park, syringes washin' up thick as oysters
Bridgeport to Bayonne – dreams so broke you can't re-
member why you love the moon, a walk with your baby

at low tide, your sneaker tracks so much graffiti sand-
blasted clean away. Rap about bizzos, scavenger bloods,
rhyme like it's something new, get yourself off on grooves

laid down by cats gone stiff in their graves & maybe
you got a chance. Let Big Joe Turner introduce you
to the blues, Ivory Joe Hunter & Bobby Nunn – hear

the Orioles warble & stomp & young girls swoon again!,
Jackie Wilson's back in school, each dingy Bijou
& Strand torn down before you were born jumpin'

like no tomorrow, even though there is. Just like
puttin' a needle to vinyl, what you do for love, there's
no kinda rush like that scratchy drawl from an ossified 78 –

Baby got you crawlin' instead of ballin'? Least no cop
boss or landlord tells you who you are. So sit down & eat
with your fathers before you, that carcass of rock 'n roll!

For B.N., WPKN Bridgeport

Homage to the Dave Clark Five

Blips from the jukebox, grooves so deep you feel each scratch
before the needle gets there – you with your gut draped

over your stool, elbows splayed across the bar's edge.
That's right, you: loosen those pudgy hands from your glass,

don't look stupid pining for someone who "says she wants
my lovin' more than any other thing (hey hey hey)" –

as if the words were ever the point! Haven't you learned
there's no such animal? That sax blowing louder

than the March wind, those drum rolls subtle as twenty mules
kicking down their stalls – they knew, those boyos,

you'd be pumping your fist before the needle picks up
a note, croaking out a tune older than that barmaid

whose name you forget & who's looking at you strange.
It's enough to be glad whole minutes at a time

for Yolanda

Chorus: Out of this Place

Brokendown parochial chords,
Chas Chandler's bass some long
obsolescent depthcharge woke
from Delta sleep with no particular
place to go, footloose & uncouth,
neither John Steel cymbal tap
louder than a dime, carfare
back to *work, work, work*
we'd kill to have again,
Alan Price's Hammond strains
muddy as a dirge when rain
came down with brickdust
that April Converse Rubber fell
imploded & defunct: wasn't
Freddy Boom Boom Cannon
dredged up where we were,
nevermind the Standells,
not even Barry & the Remains
caught that northeast wind
backdoor off the water through
the ribs of the Mystic Bridge
like Eric Burdon airing it out,
our own native tongue, still
driven back unslakened over
that same old ground, like
hauling coal to Newcastle,
like we figured it out
ourselves

"Robert, you write about Things"

Mutant New Hampshire albino spiders
always underfoot creepy as Tom De Lay
　　going about his work, drybones brittle
as dishware in the crawlspace above your
　　bed that pry into guilty dreams, petrified
fingerjoints, firstborn buried in the yard
　　deep as your family dog, that mound of
dirt an open wound framed in the stairway
　　pane, earth's the best place for grief,
buzzsaws leaping to shake your hand, no
　　more to build on there, while zombie
kinfolk never flinch, "turn to their affairs"
　　before you're even cold, turn each spring
to set the wall between 'em once again,
　　dumb as the stones themselves, as storm-
clouds shaggy as buffalo slaughtered decades
　　ago rumble & low through Vermont,
grievances from so far back you're liable
　　to catch your death, out there by yourself,
stopping by woods & nodding off or lost
　　in come frozen swamp "never to return,"
bereft as any miller moth fluttering past
　　your sight toward what is can't escape,
nothing's beneath you now, look at that
　　woodpile up ahead rotting against a
tree, bark like warped remaindered books
　　open to rain & snow who knows how
many years, that dented Ford on its side
　　in the ditch, windshield cracked like a
web, look through the glass & find your-
　　self "more truly & more strange"

Mending Wall Villanelle

Something there is that doesn't love a wall:
such knotted syntax and puns, Robert Frost.
Good fences make good neighbors after all.

Something there was that made both of you fall
back in line each March, unbent & unbossed.
Something there is that doesn't love a wall.

Something more real than frost heaves & mud, small
separate boulders that wouldn't get tossed.
Good fences make good neighbors after all.

Something more tangled than sorrows that crawl
from your unhallowed heart, when all hope's lost.
Something there is that doesn't love a wall.

Something you finally couldn't forestall
without betraying yourself, Robert Frost.
Good fences make good neighbors after all:

Somewhere you strangle those desperate calls,
Something you build on, no matter the cost.
Something there is that doesn't love a wall:
Good fences make good neighbors after all.

Black Bears in White Hills

Wake up muddy beside yourself
downwind of asphalt scents thick
    as the lower Naugatuck swollen
with benzene & sludge, roadkill
    from Beacon Falls, wake beside
treadmarks from yellow machines
    gnoshing through tree roots & rock
fast as you'd scavenge a row of
    sweetcorn, the dumpster at IGA:
what kind of hunger drove you south
    to shuffle & sniff around here, bug-
bit & gaunt through Indian Well's
    scoutpaths & scraggly pines wide
as a Route 8 median & never once
    policed, almost encroaching like
Warren Sapp on that unvarnished
    stockade fence straddling the edge
of Ward 2 but you veer off & lurch
    downhill, past Highland Acres'
8th & 9th holes, down Elm Street &
    Congress Ave., blink & it's mid-
night at Saint Joseph's Church with
    its sandblasted yellow brick grim
as the Hunter's Moon though it's al-
    ready early May & shitloads of
migrating geese squat once again in
    Trap Falls. So how'd you come to this:
shambling & pissed as Kerouac all
    over Bridgeport Ave., knocking
down Harleys that graze at the curb
    outside Porky's Café while bikers
stay nailed to their stools, feeling
    more downsized than Farrell Steel
as you gimp over railroad tracks

toward the last thing you'd want
to cross, the gravelly Housatonic,
    barely a splash at the riverbank
& you're hearsay, bodacious & near.
    Woke up beside ourselves

Cry of its Occasion

After your beard got shorter & gray, they damned you with
backhanded praise, "occasional" poet!, like all poems aren't the cry
of their occasion, that's Wallace Stevens who blew you off fifty years
ago, stuck in a payphone with only an intro from WCW: "Well, I'm
going out with the family; you wouldn't want to disturb our outing?,"
you nearly said yeah before he hung up, I'm only passing through,
only want to get your blessing, but when I said Russell would've
done worse if I'd given him pen & paper, Russell now gawked at on
Home Shopping Channel, paid to sell trinkets in malls, you told me
"Sweeney, you're too damn sane, that's what's wrong with your poems,"
sane as you were on stage in Brooklyn, scared you'd lose your gig as
Baraka roared & Orlovsky yodeled & comatose Weiners drooled,
almost scared as my mother was when I told you she was dying & you
repeated Trungpa's words to John Clellon Holmes: "if you beat the
cancer, that's good; if you die, that's good too," "I want you to tell
your mother that," but no, I never could, better his "Charnel Ground"
epigraph wiser than he ever was, all those "rugged & raw situations,
& having accepted them a part of your home ground, then some spark
of sympathy or compassion could take place; you are not in a hurry
to leave such a place immediately; you would like to face the facts,
realities of that particular world," that's what you did in *Kaddish* &
Howl better than anyone since, but when I next asked you how you
were doing: "I'm dying, that's how I'm doing; I'm doing time in this
corpse," that was November '88, a Monday so raw that Willie Horton
stayed put in Walpole Mass., your breath escaped in ragged clouds
above the concrete stoops, I pat your shoulder & said see you later but
never saw you again

4-7-97

Dugan's Edge

Grimace & squint through tobacco smoke as
pipelines explode in Iraq & Babylonian artifacts
    litter the promenades, what the hell else is new?,
Hurricane Isabel plows onshore over the Outer Banks
    & funky archaic bungalows tumble down off their
stilts into the foamy surf, who's going under next?,
    there's riptides from Truro to downeast Maine
& driftwood from who knows where washes up on
    some trashy beach nobody's painted yet, just your
grotesque lonely note for jawbones & toxic scum
    laundered & ground by the mindless sea till no one
knows which is which, no more drunk Bostonians
    roaring out "cowboy up!" like creatures that ran
down mastodons with nothing but sharpened sticks,
    what they scrawled with the great beast's blood
deep in their sacred cave's buried in glacial shale
    for nobody's eyes but theirs, that's what you're
up against, so one more shot of rotgut then & back
    to the salvage work, something untitled & un-
declaimed & cold as Ted's severed head, mortal
    as granite that's eaten away & Duane Allman's
slide guitar dug into vinyl grooves, cadences ready
    to decompose soon as you sound 'em out, that
much was always true, that hard-on you got when
    you shook her hand, you thanked her & wrote
a poem, she's still sweating up onstage "going raw
    into painful air" for us who are almost dust

(1923-2003)

for Michele Madigan Somerville

My Friend Hayden Carruth

"all poems are about other poems" (David Curtis)

And what I shall assume you shall assume, backtrack again to Walt, we can't
loaf & invite our ease without feeling guilty & sad, not at least since your friend
Jim Wright told us he's wasted his life one late summer afternoon, chickenhawk

floating home, you can spend decades erasing yourself breathing & sitting still,
beholding junipers shagged with ice & paying the wind no mind, Wright could
imagine an old stone vestal crumbling toward what he could name as cancer

metastasized, that slow smokeless burn of decay that Frost conjured up himself
on one of his lonely walks, lost in some frozen swamp, could've sung louder
all along but strangled that awful sound, so tell me again what I shall assume

who can't tell an oak from an elm, if John Edward can summon the dead you
can address Tu Fu like warm days will never cease, like I can hear you now,
tell me again how the old stand in line anxious & bitter & grim while the young

gather & roam abroad in forlorn resentful gangs, tell me again how fifty three's
a rotten time of life, threadbare end-of-winter clothes & two or three bulging
discs as we reckon our daily griefs, brothers fallen away into squalor too broke

for a root canal, tell me again how you dug up that chainsaw & set the old
sprocket down, pitted & et away, next to the butter mold, damned if you know
why, tell me again how you sat in your kitchen wolfing down store-bought pie,

tears & crumbs falling back in the tin as you reread your late friend Ray, tell me
again of the oldest killed lake & of animals gone away, it's irrevocable, all their
strungout wasted souls honking through the night, tell me again how *in a dark*

*time the existentialist flatfoot floogie stomped across the land accompanied by
a small floy floy*, everything lives & nothing is dead sang the immortal Fugs,
tell me again how you turned back your clocks & dozed off in Standard Time,

friend that I never knew, over that same old ground. *Let my snow-tracks lead
on, on. Let them, where they stop, stop. There, in mid-field.* Everything lives &
nothing is dead. *There! Whitman's skull – so elegant, sensitive, cynical, & cool*

Duet: Too Late to Stop Now

John Lee Hooker swaps lyrics with Van who's
passing sixty himself, "Gloria" *in medias res,*
they're liable to shout all night: praise to those

that wail forever like some profane choir
bad enough to croak, like their hemorrhaged
vocal cords might give up the ghost before

they both kick back, just about midnight,
& wait for that knock on their door, like
bad whiskey & poetry left 'em so deranged

they barely cast their memory back to when
browneyed or greeneyed girls, whatever,
call out their very name: G., etc., thick

as a foghorn, back through static & fumes
naked as anything Keats or Yeats hadn't
the nerve to take down when they were young

& full of themselves, mooning for Fanny
& Maud, like their verse or anyone's ripples
forward & back on the grooves of a 45,

scratchy vinyl growls, whenever the needle
drops, like they're fumbling in the grass
behind the stadium where nothing's sacred

& no one's redeemed & to paraphrase Saint
Patti Smith: Jesus died for somebody's sins
but not theirs. Now *that's* a classic

Thus I Refute Him

Crazy old bastards don't care what they say
Who won't take the other as just as fair
Kicking at any loose rocks in their way

Wonder why dawn always goes down to day?
Because it was grassy & wanted wear?
Now what's that old bastard trying to say?

On roads where the violent bear it away
You cannot petition the Lord with prayer!
Hide behind any loose rock on your way

You can gather ye rosebuds while ye may
Or mumble around the old prickly pear
Crazy old bastards don't care what they say

Or wait till the sky turns Newfoundland gray
A snowman beholding nothing that's there
Too numb to kick any rocks in your way

Once George's guitar wept gently at Shea
You're gone before anyone finds out where
Crazy old bastards mean just what they say
Mercy on any loose rocks in their way

Big Pink's For Sale

Make it a shrine & leave Garth's organ
downstairs where it belongs, underneath
    floorboards & unfrozen pipes leaky as
tears of grief welling up who knows how,
    where they bumped elbows & leaned
toward the mike while the tape crackled
    & hissed like kindling against their ears,
where they could goof & holler & hoot
    till even "Quinn the Eskimo" sounds
like a Methodist hymn, miracles never
    cease, where all their trespasses went
up in smoke & every soul shall be released
    soon as it finally figures out where it's
really coming from, whether it's Hibbing
    or Arkansas, Toronto or Saugerties,
whether it's Robbie on "Bessie Smith"
    or Richard on "Katy's Been Gone,"
his phlegmy nooseburned tenor haunting
    a guilty man's inner ears, whether
it's Levon just down the road looking
    back at that gauche pink ranch that
barely rates an AP squib too blurred for
    our middleaged eyes, they say every-
thing can be replaced & every whore's
    got his price but once in immaculate
drunkard dreams they bled on each
    track for free, forsaken but not forlorn,
anyday now you can hear Rick Danko
    yodel from Cripple Creek

Ode to Gov't Mule

They mourn Duane whose uncles broke rock on occupied Okinawa

Geezers who got their gopher gravy only from greasy granny

Grizzled young men of constant sorrow achin' to go astray

Allen Woody's underground left you makin' wicked sound

Left you askin' in all but words what's this diminished thing

If there's an original thought out there I could use it right now

Hit the ground runnin' & hear those gears grind's kinda Metallica

Jam till you chop that mountain down just with the edge of your hand

Jam from the Allman repertoire trackin' down Howlin' Wolf

Smokestack Lightnin' & Catfish Blues jammin' with Billy Cox

Jammin' with every breathin' bassist outside of Spinal Tap

All of 'em soundin' just like themselves yoked to a rebuilt Mule

Jam with Jack Bruce by the fool's moonlight thick as decrepit cream

Jam with the Ox & that guy from Phish almost like early Who

Jam till no cop or boss or landlord tells you who you are

Jam till Wal-Marts from coast to coast vote in a union shop

Jam with Mike Gordon toes in the dirt edge of the outer banks

Roger Glover layin' it down like there's smoke on the water again

Jam till all headbangin' pyrotechnics fizzle & gutter out

Separate your mind from your body & maybe you'll see the light

Jam with Meshell Ndegocello & John Cougar Mellencamp

Whole lot more than a hammer & nails to make a house a home

Jam so your roadies' sisters' boyfriends never get collared on *Cops*

No phallus or gun or Louisville Slugger or chainsaw or doubleblade axe

Jam till you damn near levitate over that same old ground

Throw your empties over the wall & watch 'em float out to sea

Who's that burnin' in effigy that can fade & reprise like the Dead

Like roundelays with Grisman & Lesh deep as a box of rain

Deadheads were known to reprise a chorus forty four verses or more

Ninemonth blew with sleeted rain & still he came not back again

Anyday now you can hear Rick Danko yodel from Cripple Creek

Weep for what little made them glad was Frost's most pathetic line

Jam through Lent & Ramadan with Scofield & Chuck Leavell

Babylonian turnpike jazz while we're bombarding Iraq

Demons steal down here comes one now lightning bolt in his teeth

Your good buddy right in your face earring & steelgray beard

Their walls are built of cannonballs their motto is don't tread on me

If you take away my pride ain't no tellin' what I might do

Do you hug your neighbor or kick his ass after the strobelights dim

Do you seek refuge & lay down at last with cutpurse & beggar & whore

Allen Woody's underground left you makin' wicked sound

Backwater accents so far gone you can't even trust your ears

If you don't know where you're goin' any road will take you there

Like haulin' coal to Newcastle like you figured it out yourself

Rainy Day Women Revisited

We'll bless you when we're breaking down your door
We'll bless you when you're on the killing floor
We'll bless you when you barely hear a sound
We'll bless you when we trash your hallowed ground
    Now we wouldn't be in such a mess
    Everybody must get blessed

We'll bless you when we put you in the stocks
We'll bless you when we fasten all the locks
We'll bless you when we knock your sisters up
We'll bless you when we blow your clinics up
    Now we wouldn't be in such a mess
    Everybody must get blessed

We'll bless you in the name of Billy Graham
We'll bless you in the name of Son of Sam
We'll bless you in the name of Tim McVeigh
We'll bless you when your gods have flown away
    Now we wouldn't be in such a mess
    Everybody must get blessed

We'll bless you when you swear that we were right
We'll bless you when you grovel through the night
We'll bless you when we throw you down the well
We'll bless you when we cast you into hell
    Now we wouldn't be in such a mess
    Everybody must get blessed

Heartland Nada

Heartland's so big we had to build walls so nobody
gets inside, no stone left uncast or unturned, no more un-
graven slabs too bad to haul away, nothing but goddamn
grovellers, might as well fuck out of doors or swear off
mesquite & pork, nothing tastes good enough, if freedom's
just another word for nothing left to lose then nothing's
worth walling out, we're nothing but gangbanging knuckle-
heads, bitches, snitches & screws, Wal-Mart greeters &
rottweiler trainers & cocksucking entrepreneurs, bornagain
skinheads & chickenhawk priests & third generation scabs,
telemarketing overseers & Heritage bugeyed blondes,
nothing but postal Apache grunts, we're in their sights
down in the yard where there's nothing but time to kill,
where we pump iron & keep taking names & gaze through
the razorwire as rotorblades beat overhead, rolling thunder
from Yucatan, nothing but tumbleweed near the high-
voltage chainlink fence

Cold Pastoral

Skynard's righteous lead guitars
made Yankees wave the Stars & Bars;
that "Sweet Home Alabama" rant
struck motherlode for Ron Van Zant

Downhome rock from Muscle Shoals
cleansing all our wayward souls
pure as gypsies soaked in rain
& pharmaceutical cocaine

One day we'll crash unafraid
through that final barricade
where no pissed off Southern Man's
sworn again to take his stand

No more bloodshed for the Cause,
marchers blasted with a hose;
no more lynchings, no more hate,
no more ghosts of Watergate

But Jesse Helms & David Duke
don't make every redneck puke
& Pat Buchanan rides again
weekday nights on CNN

So listen up to old Neil Young
& each self-righteous verse he sung:
when churches burn & bullwhips crack
even dead bands watch their back

Holy Icons of Mother Russia

   Christ himself allowed Saint Luke to paint his sacred portrait
so there's no idolatry, just honest craftsmanship, icons on wood
a thousand years old hacked from deserving trees, wood that
serfs might've gladly burned mounted for public display, hung
for agnostics & worse, every heart-shaped countenance utterly
disengaged. You can stand with them like Pasternak & not
be the wiser man, not till you face your shame, flog an already
broken horse or beg for your worthless life but witness that dread
ascent, however you kneel or crawl. How can they float above
altar & cross on solar vermilion rays? How can that primitive
blood-orange light seep from their flaking pores? How can they
breathe those turquoise hues without getting vertigo? They're
not human, those martyrs & saints, those translucent Roswell
eyes, they see Chernobyl & Babi Yar, the gulags you resurrect
no matter your tongue or creed. An innocent system & a guilty
defendant, that's what John Ashcroft said, you can believe
Raskolnikov opened his wretched heart. You can look through
them like cold stained glass warmed by the Arctic sun, where
suffering's sacrosanct. You can appreciate anything
executed so well

     for Patricia Elizabeth Sweeney

Further

Left on the shoulder to wallow & grope,
that rickety Prankster bus never had brakes
or reverse, too far gone to catch your breath
in the wake of its funky exhaust roaring back
at you like surf, rushing back through your
bloodstream again quickening underground,
through your nine digits & raggedy lungs
holier than a sleve: inspiration burns out
fast as what you can suck from a pipe,
each meandering forlorn jam kickstarted
on a whim & rode till the fumes gave out,
every dark uncharted chord wrung from
those dewy strings like cloudbursts inside
your skull, even bootlegs yet unearthed
fresher than Workingman's Dead, blind-
sides you every time: none of it echoes
long enough for anyone else to know where
you'd lay down & take your rest, where
you rose up to plug into sound too keen
to be heard again, notes you played once
& forgot, feedback stranger than Cassady's
& deep as a box of rain. Where you rose up
& stuck out your thumb

August 1995

68

The Last Cracker

August Wilson's eleventh play we'll reconstruct scene by scene from mud
& survivor's guilt, those postdiluvian blues, we can appropriate anything
below Lake Pontchartrain. We can scavenge 9th Ward streets for spittoons
& bassinets too funky to be redeemed, mangled umbrellas & chandeliers,
soiled Quatorze chairs—one humongous teeming set to feel we were truly
there after the levees broke. Next we can scour the Superdome for scofflaws
& indigents who'd die for a Poland Spring before the damn barn implodes—
there's a cast of thousands here who won't get an audience until they grow
tres deranged. We can't hear 'em keen or declaim unless they're apocryphal
or irrefutable as Phyllis Montana LeBlanc, fundamental as the flood
that swallowed up every soul that crawled below Mount Ararat—soon all
rivers surge into one & e-coli runs through it, muskrat gumbo & fossil fuel,
putrefied crawfish & squid. Once the waters recede for good we'll build
a proscenium arch that spans the great sewage ditch bisecting Cite Soleil—
there's still driftwood from unlaunched rafts, machetes & M-16's, necklaced
Creoles & staggering zombies, shoeless mown down like cane. There's been
drama for five hundred years across every latitude besieged by the rain & sun—
stone Fat Tuesday *danses macabres* where maggots still boogie hard deep in
their swollen hosts, histrionic trumpeters that don't rate a horse-drawn hearse,
unpurged stragglers without a prayer limping for higher ground like Sherman
was at their heels who elsewhere struck a note too human to be expunged:
War is cruelty & you cannot refine it. But, my dear sirs, when peace does come,
you can call on me for anything. Then I will share with you the last cracker.
We can appropriate tragedy down to those lame *mots justes*

How Benjy Saw Rodney King

He was it & they were hitting, nightsticks & boot-
   heels when he roll over, he was wiggling
on the asphalt elbows bend upside his head,
   knotted & churn around the circle fire-
light rose & fall, redblue siren whiplash
   its shadow still my tongue kept hush,
he was flapping like a catfish prod on a barb-
   wire fence, he was rolling like a melon
kicked over redblue coals, they weren't hitting
   they wouldn't stop till the circle broke,
steer its shadow rosen & fallen, whipgnash
   prone & cuff, my lungs could bellow
my tongue kept hush my windpipe gaggle
   & burn, those dumb eyeballs those
redblue sockets flashing like Polaroid,
   like firelight in the asylum after
that evening sun lay me dribble & curl:
   they were hitting & he was it

Hypothetical Questions, 1971

...if you're lucky one day you'll find out
Where it is you're really coming from
  The Basement Tapes

   Let's say you've got your thumb out
halfway down Western Ave. where road
widens to highway, toes almost numb in
the April chill as the sun dips closer to
the pinetops, & suppose a metallic blue
Volkswagen pulls over & you get in,
the driver barely nodding as you ask
"Down the road a bit?", nodding really
to a scratchy drawl that might be Dylan's
coming from the tape deck: would you
feel strange being driven so far with no
words between you but the music on
the tape, songs more weathered than
any saltbox you pass coming into Salem
but Dylan's inflections making you feel
your life hadn't slipped past you yet?,
& would you get spooked when the VW
stops right at the corner you'd have told
the driver to if you'd been paying attention,
just a nod as the last light catches his wire-
rimmed glasses, you forgetting his face
soon as he's back on the road, driving
north into the darkness? Didn't think so

Allen Ginsberg's Sneakers

My own life, scandal! Lazy bum! Secondhand royal scarlet ties & Yves
St. Laurent Salvation Army blazers

    Think now of Walt in his opera suit & his widebrimmed fancy hat &
how you wept alone in China at his "desperado farewell," "who touches
this book touches a man," of Burroughs who followed a season behind
in his undertaker's garb, deadpan to the end, his Kansas backyard
shotgun art splintered through MTV, through Nike & U2's "End of the
World," "no choice but to write my way out," of Michelle Kerouac beat
as *memere*, "when you go there use my name," peasant hands gnarled as
her father's, beaten as Lowell itself on stillborn Saturday nights when
lattice-grilles strangle the last drop of cheer from smokeglass storefront
bars & no roman candles flower like spiders & no one's there to go
"aww," of Huncke already gone a year who took the shirt off your back,
who got you busted & trucked off to Bellevue but who you always
took in no matter how strungout & "heartsick alone," "not till the sun
rejects you do I," all your company's out on parole from their stretch
on the Charnel Ground, their corpses nothing more than cells they
trashed to keep half sane, "smeared graffiti on the walls & stopped the
toilets up, set the mattresses on fire" & chanted "all gone all gone all
overgone all gone sky-high now old mind so Ah!" like nothing gets left
behind, but my friend Mia's painting your sneakers & giving the canvas
to me, some old photo from *Life* magazine that caught you on the fly
'twixt *Kaddish* & *White Shroud*, she'll make those ratty black & white
Keds glow like plutonium, they'll have a half-life long enough to say
to your unborn sons just as I walk the Lower East Side this wind-swept
April dusk, so will all of you walk, just as I climb these creaky stairs to
my rent-controlled drafty rooms, so will all of you climb, just as I lay
in my narrow bed & nod off forevermore, so will all of you nod, you
can walk again in my shoes reading those scattered poems butchered
out of my body "good to eat a thousand years," you were there & I'll be
with you under bootsoles & grass, it all goes back to Walt, I'll be there
waiting for you

An Evening with the Allman Brothers

Back in the drafty Fillmore East you could jam till the sun came up

First there is a mountain then there is no mountain then there is

Catch your breath in the alleyway & sweat in the cold March light

Man you could damn near levitate over that same old ground

Throw your empties over the wall & watch 'em float out to sea

Bygone Macon graveyard nights you'd be courting Elizabeth Reed

What thou lovest well remains drinkin' in some crosstown bar

No phallus or gun or Louisville Slugger or chainsaw or doubleblade axe

Nothin' like those old fatigues but now you lay down alone

Sonic exhaust at Watkins Glen when you broke bread with the Dead

This is an old true story called I must've did somebody wrong

You could jam longer than the Dead way back at Hundred Year Hall

Inspiration burns out fast as what you can suck from a pipe

I don't own the clothes I'm wearin' & the road goes on forever

Late October afternoons you'd be bleeding all over the road

No one hears his lonely sighs there are no blankets where he lies

No repossessed campers on cinderblocks gone up the Merrimack

Dickey at Pinecrest all by himself fumbling the verse to *Blue Sky*

Feel free to sing along if you know the words if not just hum

Our family stammers until half mad we come to speech at last

Could've sung louder all along but strangled that awful sound

Dinner theater acoustic gigs you'd be pickin' like no tomorrow

Could've been any one of us boys scattered through April winds

Blow on your hands before you punch in high on the rubber & glue

Aprils when Fenway was one quarter full & Converse ran graveyard shifts

Walk yourself backwards to Rock Valley Ave. & watch the front porch collapse

Like downtrodden bornagain trash tied to the whippin' post

Down forever in that groove what never was never sounds better

Wish I was free of that slaving meatwheel safe in heaven dead

Heavy rotation on VH 1 with Skynyrd & Stevie Ray Vaughan

That Sweethome Alabama rant struck motherlode for Ron Van Zant

Closing out Jimmy's second inaugural nobody noddin' off

Pat Buchanan rides again weekday nights on CNN

No lone brother in Massachusetts prone & impaled with a flag

Brothers fallen away into squalor too broke for a root canal

Crawl under your car all day Saturday nothin' but a wrench

Listening again to *Les Brers in A Minor* doesn't assuage me at all

John Lee Hooker sat in on Duane's *Crawlin' Jurassic Blues*

Already sure it's enough to be glad whole minutes at a time

Crawlin' down avenues never condemned nevermind gentrified

Still can't remember these last thirty years just what they're holdin' me for

We'll reach it & we'll all be singin' & we'll all be friends

Back in that drafty alleyway you'd be giving up all you had

Had ourselves a fine evening: Berry Oakley…Dickey Betts…

Somebody's always after you to fuck up & blame yourself

Butch Trucks…Jai Johnny Johnson…Gregg Allman…

Breathe again in the early light & load the Econoline van

I'm Duane Allman thank you

for Robert, & in memory of Bill (1938-2003)
& Jim (1932-2006)

About the Author

Michael Sweeney was born in Malden, Massachusetts, and grew up in neighboring Everett. He graduated from Salem State College, the University of Bridgeport, and Brooklyn College, where he studied with Allen Ginsberg and Susan Fromberg Schaeffer; he also trained in Isshinryu Modes Karate, attaining the rank of nidan. Twice nominated for the Pushcart Prize, Sweeney teaches at Fairfield University, and lives in Shelton, Connecticut, with his wife Patricia. *In Memory of the Fast Break* has been a finalist for the Backwaters Prize (Backwaters Press) and Nicholas Roerich Prize (Story Line Press).

Printed in the United States
201942BV00006B/1-51/P

9 781891 386718